_____

To

_____

From

_____

Date

# Standard
# BIBLE STORYBOOK SERIES
# MIRACLES
## OF JESUS

## Retold by Carolyn Larsen

Standard®
PUBLISHING

Cincinnati, Ohio

Published by Standard Publishing, Cincinnati, Ohio
www.standardpub.com
Copyright © 2012 by Standard Publishing

Printed in: China

Project editors: Elaina Meyers, Dawn A. Medill, and Marcy Levering
Cover design: Dale Meyers

Illustrations from Standard Publishing's Classic Bible Art Collection

ISBN 978-0-7847-3526-8

Library of Congress Cataloging-in-Publication Data

Larsen, Carolyn, 1950-
  Miracles of Jesus / retold by Carolyn Larsen.
    p. cm.
  ISBN 978-0-7847-3526-8
1.  Jesus Christ--Miracles--Juvenile literature. 2.  Bible stories, English.
N.T. Gospels.  I. Title.
  BT366.3.L37 2012
  232.9'55--dc23
                              2011051572

17  16  15  14  13  12      1  2  3  4  5  6  7  8  9

# JESUS TEACHES BY HEALING

Jesus' tender care for people who are hurting showed in the many times He healed the sick or injured. His reputation as a healer spread and people began bringing their sick friends and neighbors to be healed by Jesus. And when they did, Jesus healed them. Sometimes He even went the next step and raised someone from the dead. These miracles showed God's loving heart and His amazing power!

## Jesus Heals a Blind Man *John 9:1-34*

J esus and His disciples were walking along a road one day when they saw a man who was blind. The man had never been able to see because he was born blind. His disciples stopped and looked at the man, then they asked Jesus a question. "Master, why was this man born blind? Was it because of his sins or those of his parents?"

"He wasn't born blind because of sin at all," Jesus answered. "It was so that God's power could be seen in him. All of us need to carry out God's work while we're here because the time is short. While I am here in this world, I am the light of the world."

Then Jesus bent down and spit into the dirt. He made mud and spread the mud over the blind man's eyes. Then He said, "Go wash the mud off in the Pool of Siloam." The

man did what Jesus told him to do and when he came back he could see!

The people who had known the man who was blind were amazed. "Is this the same man who has been blind his whole life?" they asked each other. "How can he see now?" they wondered. Some even thought that it must be a different man, but he sure looked like

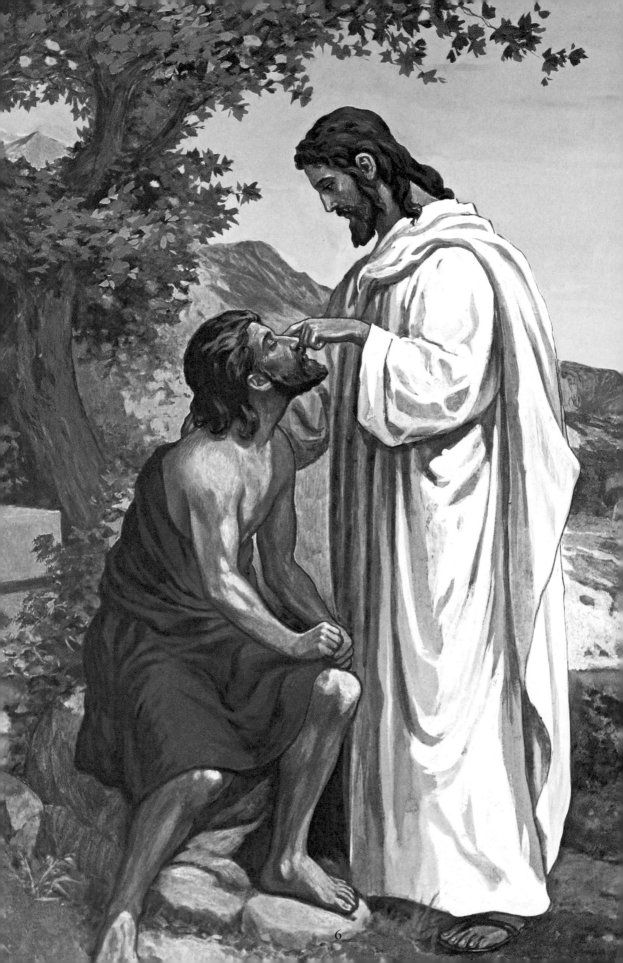

the man they had always known.

The man kept telling them, "It's me! It's really me!"

"Who healed you?" they asked. "How can you see now?"

He explained to them about Jesus putting the mud on his eyes and telling him to wash it off; he could see after that. They wanted to know where Jesus went but the man didn't know. So they took the man to see the Pharisees. It just so happened that Jesus healed the man on the Sabbath and the Pharisees did not approve of that since work was not to be done on that day. When the Pharisees asked the man about what had happened to him, he explained the entire story to them.

Some of the Pharisees said, "Jesus cannot be from God or He wouldn't be doing work on the Sabbath." But others wondered how an ordinary man could do such an amazing miracle. So the Pharisees didn't agree with each other. They asked the man again what had happened and once again he told them the story. Then they asked him who he thought Jesus was.

"He's a prophet," the man answered.

The Pharisees did not want to believe that Jesus had performed a miracle. Then they went to talk to the man's parents. "Was your son really born blind?" they asked. "If so, why can he see now?"

"Yes, he was born blind," they answered. "We do not know why he can see now. We do not know who healed him. He is an adult and can speak for himself, so talk with him about it." The parents were afraid the Pharisees would kick them out of the temple if they even hinted that Jesus might be the Messiah.

So the Pharisees went back to the man and asked him the same questions. Once again, he answered in the same way. Then he asked, "Why do you keep asking me the same questions? Do you want to become Jesus' disciples too?" That really made them angry!

"We know that God spoke to Moses and we follow his teachings. We don't know where this Jesus came from."

"Well," the man said, "no one has ever been able to open the eyes of a man born blind and God doesn't do what sinners tell Him to do. So He must be from God."

The Pharisees threw the man out of the temple.

# Down Through the Roof

*Matthew 9:1-7; Mark 2:1-12; Luke 5:18-25*

**J**esus came to the city of Capernaum and a large crowd gathered at the house where He was staying. Some people wanted to hear Jesus teach about God. Some were just curious about Him. Some of the religious leaders were there just to keep an eye on Him. Very soon the house was so full that not even one more person could get in. Jesus began teaching about God. Outside the house four men came up. They each were holding a corner of a cot that carried a friend of theirs who couldn't walk. They wanted Jesus to heal their friend. But the house was so crowded they couldn't even get inside the door. So the friends carried the cot up to the roof of the house, dug a hole in the roof all the way through to the room where Jesus was, and lowered their friend down into the room. He came down right in front of Jesus. Seeing the extreme faith of these four friends, Jesus spoke to the man who was paralyzed, "Son, your sins are forgiven."

The religious leaders in the room were furious. "How can He forgive sins?" they asked. "What gives Him the right to do that? Only God can forgive sins."

Jesus knew what they were thinking so He said, "Is it easier to say, 'Pick up your mat and walk?' or to say, 'Your sins are forgiven?' I will prove that I have the authority to forgive sins." Then he turned to the man again and said, "Get up. Pick up your cot and go home. You are healed."

Right away the man jumped up and picked up his own cot and pushed his way through the crowd of people in the room. The people were amazed. They said, "We've never seen anything like this!"

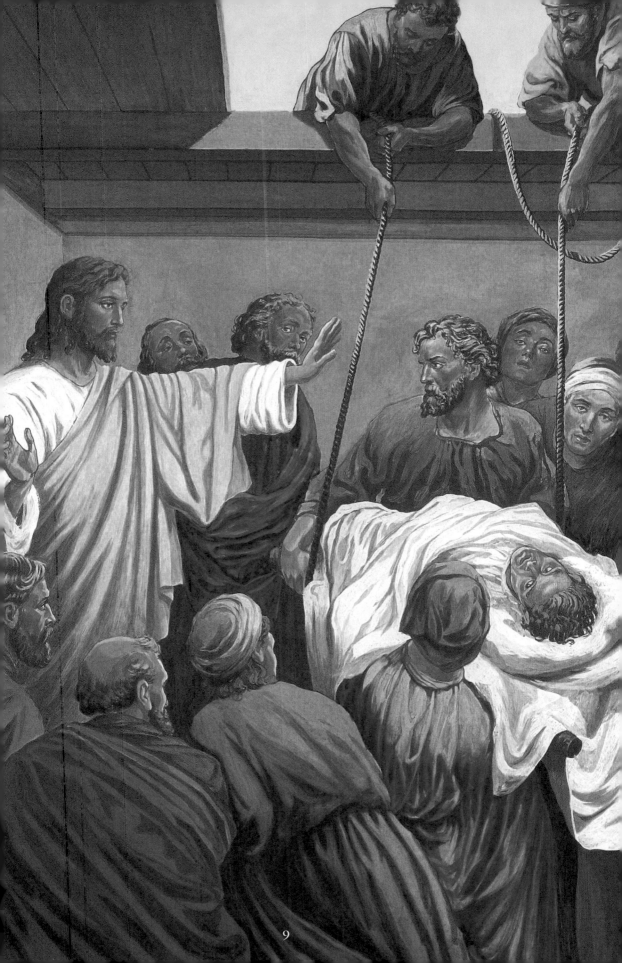

# The Son of a Government Official

*John 4:46-54*

Jesus traveled from town to town, teaching and challenging people to follow God. He also healed sick people and did other miracles. His very first miracle happened in Cana when He changed water to wine at a wedding party. There was a man in a nearby city who worked in the government. He was important and powerful. The man had a son who was very sick and when he heard that Jesus was in town he came to

see Him. He begged Jesus to come to Capernaum with him to heal his son. The boy was so sick that he was very near death.

Jesus said, "Do I have to keep doing miracles in order for you people to believe in me?"

"Please, please," the official said, "please come with me before my son dies!"

Jesus said, "Go on home. Your son will be fine." The man believed Jesus and started home.

While the official was on his way his servants came and met him. They told him that his son was well so he shouldn't worry. He asked them when the little boy had begun to improve. They told him, "About one o'clock yesterday his fever suddenly disappeared."

The man realized that was the exact time that Jesus had told him, "Go on home. Your son will be fine." Right then the officer and everyone in his house believed in Jesus.

# The Servant of a Roman Officer

*Matthew 8:5-13; Luke 7:1-10*

An officer in the Roman army came to Jesus one time and begged for His help. "Sir, my servant is paralyzed. He can't get out of bed and he is in terrible pain. Please help him."

"All right," Jesus said, "I will come to your house with you and help him."

"I am not worthy of having You come to my house," the officer said. "Just say the word right now and I know that my servant will be healed. I understand about authority because I am under the authority of my superiors and I have people under my authority. I only need to tell them to do something and they do it."

Jesus was amazed at the faith this man had in Him. He said, "I have never seen faith like this in all of Israel." Then He turned to the Roman officer and said, "Go on home. You believed that I would heal your servant and I have done so." The officer found out later that the servant was healed right at that moment!

# Jesus Heals Ten Men *Luke 17:11-19*

**J**esus was walking to Jerusalem. In Bible times most people walked everywhere they went. As usual, a large crowd of people was walking with Jesus. Just as the crowd crossed the border between Galilee and Samaria, Jesus noticed a group of men standing some distance away. They all suffered from the disease called leprosy. Leprosy was very contagious, so the law stated that when a person had it, he had to leave his home and live in a leper colony. That meant the sick people could not live at home with their families. This group that Jesus noticed was a group of ten men who all had leprosy. When they saw that Jesus had noticed them, all ten of them began shouting to Him, "Please, Jesus, have mercy on us!"

Jesus calmly told them to go and show themselves to the priests. The men may not have understood why Jesus said to do that, but they all took off running toward the temple. As they were running, their bodies were miraculously healed of the leprosy! Completely healed!

One of the men stopped right in his tracks when he realized that he was healed. He turned around and came back to Jesus, fell down on his knees, and said, "Praise God! I'm healed!" He put his face right down on the ground and just kept thanking Jesus for healing him. This particular man wasn't even a Jew. He was a Samaritan.

Of course Jesus was happy about the man's gratitude, but He said, "Didn't I heal ten men? Where are the other nine? Why did only one man return to thank me?" Then Jesus told the man to get up off the ground and go home because his faith had made him well.

# Lazarus *John 11:1-44*

J esus had a very good friend in Bethany. His name was Lazarus and he had two sisters, Mary and Martha. When Lazarus got sick, his sisters sent a message to Jesus asking Him to come to their home.

But when Jesus got the message

He said, "Lazarus won't die from this illness. It is for God's glory." Even though Jesus loved Lazarus and his sisters very much, He didn't go to Bethany right away. He waited about two days, then said, "Let's go to Judea" (that's where Bethany was).

His disciples didn't think it was a good idea to go to Judea. "Master, don't You remember that the religious leaders in Judea threatened to kill You just a few days ago? It isn't safe to go there."

"Our friend Lazarus is sleeping. We must go there and wake him," Jesus answered.

"Wait a minute," the disciples said, "if he is sleeping then that means he is getting better from his sickness." They thought Jesus was saying that Lazarus was resting, but He was actually saying that Lazarus had died.

"I am trying to tell you that Lazarus has died. I'm actually glad that I wasn't there to help him because now you will see God's power and believe in me," Jesus said.

They all left for Bethany and when they got there Jesus was told that Lazarus had died and been buried

four days before. Many friends and neighbors were at Mary and Martha's house offering their support and sympathy. Someone told Martha that Jesus was coming down the road and she ran out to meet Him. Mary stayed at home with the other people. Martha ran up to Jesus and said, "Lord, if You had been here my brother would not have died. Still, I know that God will do whatever You ask."

"Your brother will rise again," Jesus said.

"Yes, I know that when everyone rises at the resurrection he will rise too," Martha said.

"I am the resurrection and the life," Jesus said. "People who believe in me will live forever, even though they die. They will have eternal life for believing in me. Do you believe this, Martha?"

"Yes, I do believe," Martha said. "I have always believed that You are the Messiah, the Son of God." Then she went back home to her sister. "Mary, Jesus is here and He wants to see you," she told Mary. Immediately Mary went to Jesus.

"My brother would not have died if You had come," Mary said to Jesus. She began to cry and when Jesus saw her grief He was very upset. Some of the people wondered why Jesus hadn't come and helped Lazarus because they knew He could do miracles. He had healed blind people before.

"Where have you buried him?" Jesus asked. Someone told Him where Lazarus was buried and Jesus began to cry. He approached the tomb where Lazarus was buried and said, "Roll the stone away!"

Martha said, "He's been buried for four days and will smell terrible!"

"I told you that you would see God's glory if you believed, didn't I?" Jesus said. So some of the men rolled the stone aside. Jesus looked up to Heaven and said, "Father, thank You for hearing my prayers." Then He shouted, "Lazarus, come out!" All the people there were amazed when Lazarus walked out of the tomb, still wrapped in the burial cloths. Jesus said, "Unwrap him and let him go!"

# JESUS TEACHES BY DOING MIRACLES

Jesus wanted everything He said and did to point people to God. More than anything He wanted people to know God, trust Him, obey Him, and love Him. Sometimes Jesus showed God's amazing power by doing miracles; things that no average human being could do. The people who saw these miracles often believed that Jesus was truly God's Son, the Messiah!

## Jesus Calms the Storm

*Matthew 8:23-27; Mark 4:35-41; Luke 8:22-25*

Everywhere Jesus went a large crowd of people followed Him. He spent His days teaching them, healing them, and talking with them. He got very little rest. One day, He had been teaching all day and at evening time He said to His disciples, "Let's cross to the other side of this lake." So they all got into a boat and began sailing across the lake. Some of the people in the crowd got into other boats and followed them.

Jesus went to the back of the boat to lay down. He was so tired from the long day of teaching that He fell asleep. When the boat got out to the middle of the lake, a terrible storm suddenly blew in. The wind blew the boat around and the waves crashed against it. The disciples were terrified. They thought they were going to die out there on the lake! They frantically went to Jesus and said, "Teacher, help us! We're going to drown out here!"

Jesus got up and looked at the waves, "Be still!" He said. Immediately the wind stopped blowing and the waves calmed down. Everything was quiet. Then Jesus turned to His disciples and asked, "Why were you so afraid? Don't you have faith in me?"

All of His disciples were amazed at Jesus' power. "Who is this man?" they asked each other. "Even the wind and waves obey Him!"

# Jairus's Daughter _Mark 5:21-43_

**A**s usual, Jesus was surrounded by people who wanted Him to heal their sick or do other miracles for them. Jairus, a leader of one local synagogue, heard that Jesus was nearby, and he came out to see Him, and fell at Jesus' feet. "Sir, my little girl is very sick. She is about to die. Please come to my house and heal her," the man begged.

Jesus started to go with the man as the crowd pushed in around Him. A woman who had been sick for twelve years was in the crowd. She had so much faith in Jesus that she believed that if she could just touch the hem of His robe she would be healed. So she reached through the crowd and grabbed His robe. Jesus stopped immediately and asked, "Who touched my clothes?" His disciples couldn't believe He asked that because there were people all around Him. "I felt power go out from me," Jesus said. "Who touched me?"

The woman stepped up and admitted that she did it. "I just wanted to be well because I have been sick for so long," she said.

Jesus was touched by her faith. "Your faith has made you well," He said.

While Jesus was talking to her,

Jairus's servant came up and said, "Don't bother Jesus anymore. It's too late. Your daughter is dead." But Jesus ignored this and went on to Jairus's house.

"Don't be afraid. Just trust me," He told Jairus. He only let Peter, James, and John go with Him to Jairus's house. When He arrived there, people were crying and sobbing. "Why all this crying?" He asked. "The girl isn't dead. She is just sleeping." The people made fun of Him but He told them all to leave the house. Then He took Jairus, the girl's mother, and His three disciples with Him into the girl's room. He took her hand and said, "Get up, little girl." The girl got up right away and began walking around the room! Her parents were so thankful and amazed. Jesus told them to give the girl something to eat.

# Jesus Feeds 5,000

*Matthew 14:15-21; Mark 6:35-44; Luke 9:12-17; John 6:1-13*

J esus was trying to get some alone time but everywhere He went large crowds of people followed Him. He and His disciples got on a boat to get away from the crowds for a while, but when the boat docked He found that the people had rushed across land and were there waiting for Him. He was filled with love for the people so He healed the

people who were sick that they had brought to Him and He taught them about God. The afternoon passed quickly and when evening came the disciples came to Jesus and said, "Send the people away so they can go into the villages and get food."

But Jesus had another idea. He said, "No, you get food for them."

"That's just not possible," the disciples said. "We don't have enough money to buy food for all these people."

"Do you have any food at all?" Jesus asked.

"There is a young boy in the crowd who has a lunch of five loaves of bread and two fish. He says he will give it to us. But it isn't enough to feed all these people."

"Get the young boy's lunch for me," Jesus said. "Then have all the people sit down in groups of fifty." Jesus took the loaves and fish and lifted them up toward Heaven and asked God to bless it. He began breaking the fish and bread into pieces and the disciples passed it out to the people. There were over 5,000 people in that crowd. Everyone had all they wanted to eat. When they had finished eating, the disciples picked up the leftover food. They collected twelve baskets of leftover food and it all came from five loaves of bread and two fish!

# Jesus Walks on Water

*Matthew 14:22-33; Mark 6:47-51; John 6:16-21*

One time when Jesus had been teaching all day He needed some time alone. So He sent His disciples on to Bethsaida by boat. Meanwhile, He went up into the hills to be alone and pray.

During the night the disciples were in a boat out in the middle of the lake and Jesus was still on the land. The disciples were rowing hard into the wind and the waves were bouncing their little boat all around.

At about three o'clock in the morning, Jesus, walking on top of the water, came to His friends! He started to walk right past them but when His friends saw Him they screamed because they thought He was a ghost! But Jesus said, "Calm down. It's me. Don't be afraid."

Just then, Peter called to Him, "Lord, if that's really You out there on the water, call to me and I will walk on the water too!"

"OK," Jesus said, "Come on."

Peter jumped out of the boat and began walking on the water toward Jesus. But when Peter looked around at the big waves surrounding him, he was afraid and he started to sink into the water. "Save me!" he called to Jesus.

Instantly, Jesus reached out His hand and grabbed Peter. "You don't have much faith," Jesus said to him. "Why did you doubt me?"

Then He climbed into the boat with the disciples and the wind calmed down right away. The disciples were amazed, and said " Yes, You are the Son of God!"

# A LOOK AT GLORY

Jesus' teachings and the miracles He did often moved people to believe that He is the Messiah and Savior of the world. His twelve disciples spent pretty much all their time with Him for the 3 ½ years of Jesus' earthly ministry. He especially became very close to Peter, James, and John. These men got to see Jesus' heavenly glory!

# The Transfiguration
*Matthew 17:1-13; Mark 9:2-13; Luke 9:28-36*

J esus knew that His ministry on earth was winding down. The end of His life was getting closer and closer. His disciples didn't seem to understand that though. After one particularly hard talk Jesus had with them He took Peter, James, and John with Him up on a high mountain. No one else was with them; just the four of them were alone on the mountain.

Peter, James, and John were

amazed because as they watched, Jesus' appearance changed completely. His face shone as bright as the sun. They could barely look at Him because His face was so bright. His clothing even changed from His normal appearance. He was suddenly wearing robes that were brilliant white! The disciples had never seen anything like it! Suddenly, two more men were

there with Jesus. The disciples recognized them as Moses and Elijah. The two old prophets began to talk with Jesus about how He was going to finish God's plan for Him by dying in Jerusalem. Peter was so completely overwhelmed with the glory of what he saw—two famous old prophets and Jesus glowing brightly—that he blurted out, "This is wonderful. It is amazing! If You want, I will build three memorials right now to honor this experience. One will be for You, one for Moses, and one for Elijah."

While Peter was speaking, a cloud came down from Heaven and settled over them. Peter, James, and John couldn't see anything at all through the cloud. They heard a voice coming from Heaven that said, "This is my beloved Son and I am very happy

with Him. Listen closely to Him." The disciples fell down on the ground, covered their eyes, and were terrified.

When the cloud lifted, Moses and Elijah were gone. Jesus came over to His friends and told them to get up. "Don't be afraid," He said. "Don't tell anyone what you have seen here until I have risen from the dead."

The disciples were not sure what He meant by that. But they did have a question, "Why do the religious leaders insist that Elijah has to return before the Messiah comes?"

Jesus said, "Elijah is coming first to set everything straight. But the truth is that he already came but no one recognized him. They mistreated him and soon the Son of Man will be mistreated too."

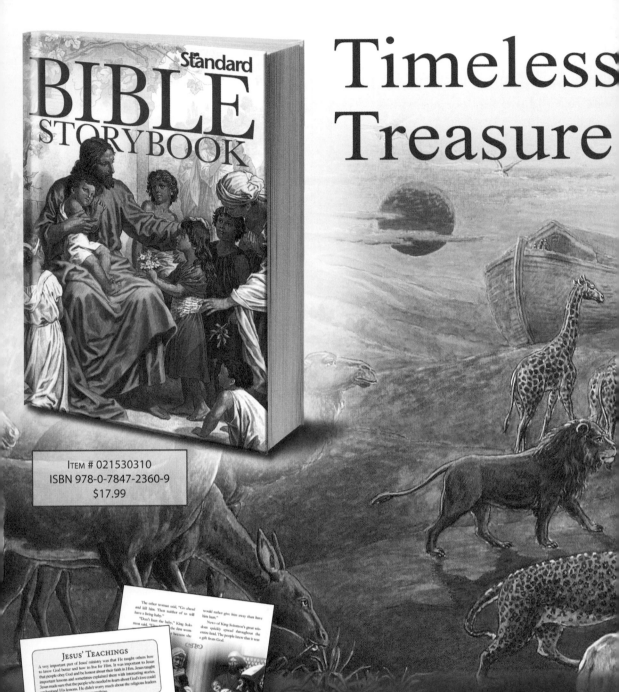